CLOSE TO THE SHORE

POEMS BY

Jacqueline Marcus

Michigan State University Press
East Lansing

Michigan State University Press
East Lansing, Michigan 48823-5245

Printed and bound in the United States of America.

08 07 06 05 04 03 02   1 2 3 4 5 6 7 8 9 10

LIBRARY OF CONGRESS CATALOGING-IN-PUBLICATION DATA

Marcus, Jacqueline,
Close to the shore / Jacqueline Marcus.
   p. cm.
ISBN 0-87013-608-9 (pbk.: alk. paper)
1. Title.
PS3613.A3674 C57 2002
813'.6 — DC21

                                    2002006807

Cover and interior design by Valerie Brewster,
   Scribe Typography, Port Townsend, WA
Cover artwork is *View of the Sea at Scheveningen* by Vincent
   Van Gogh and is used courtesy of Van Gogh Museum
   Enterprises

Visit Michigan State University Press on the World Wide Web at:

                    www.msupress.msu.edu

for Richard
& for my mother
with gratitude and love

ACKNOWLEDGMENTS

The author gratefully acknowledges the following publications where these poems first appeared.

The Antioch Review: "At the End of the Day I Listen to Bach"
The Kenyon Review: "No Other Heaven"
The Ohio Review: "Logos"; "Why Eros Will Not Return"
The Wallace Stevens Journal: "Driving into Town with Franz Joseph Haydn"
The Journal: "Absolution through the Cello"
Poetry International: "Wood-Carved Horse in Autumn"
5 AM: "September"
College English: "Vincent Van Gogh's Mulberry Tree"; "The Drowning"; "Thanksgiving"
The Literary Review: "Metamorphosis"
Hayden's Ferry Review: "Old Peasant, 1903"
The Sycamore Review: "Sycamore Bay"
Passages North: "Los Osos Valley Road"
Mid-American Review: "Remembering Giotto"
Poet Lore: "Long Day's Journey"; "Simone Weil on Easter Morning"
Cider Press Review: "The Other Side of the Night"; "Small Tree"
The Bellingham Review: "Waters of the Sun"
Faultline: "Privilege"; "Being"
ThreeCandles.org: "October"; "Korinthiakòs Kòlpos"
Iris: "Coup de Grâce"
The Seattle Review: "Another Chance"
Appalachia: "At Big Sur"
Ascent: "Take Five"
SamsaraQuarterly.net: "Kafka and Milena"; "Magenta in Fall"
Cafe Solo: "A Chorus of Rains"

ANTHOLOGIES
1997 Anthology of Magazine Verse & Yearbook of American Poetry: "Absolution through the Cello"
Red Hen Press Anthology 2002

CHAPBOOK
White Heron Press: 1999 "Absolution through the Cello"

Contents

ONE

TWO

THREE

CLOSE TO THE SHORE

One

There is no return.
        L'infinita venuta del tutto is an illusion.

Nobody is here. Only strange people
        hurrying after their strange affairs.
        ALEKSANDER WAT

Man cannot live without a permanent trust in
something indestructible in himself.
        FRANZ KAFKA

Logic and sermons never convince,
The damp of the night drives deeper into my soul.
        WALT WHITMAN

Absolution through the Cello

So now my dear cello,
light of darkness—sad, sweet bass—
what will you play for me tonight? What quiet reminder
through the foghorn's pulse?
                            The room is senseless,
and everyone needs their comfort from time to time.

Like old Père Goriot,
drinking his stale tea in a cracked cup
with winter coming on from the dolorous trees,
what bass sound could borrow such weathered clothes,
                                          such a poor moon,

begging for a taste of water?

Will you sing of the leaves, grey and deadly in the streets?
How strange to think of yourself in this way—
an old man, like Hemingway's figure who leans into the candle
        of a late night café,
how this cello illuminates my darkest fear,
my best recollection, my sun-drenched dreams, clean as a sheet,
pinned to the sea-air to dry.

How strange to think of my whole life like a secret grave—
a night with the lapping waves, my *beautiful* cello,
the moon, brushing my blond hair,
the shadows of ancient trees that reach for me and want me,
poor, sad soldiers...

You sing as if I were truly with them,
living and partly living,

like the women of Canterbury waiting for their saintly Bishop.
You ask for my confession, dear, sad cello.

                              But I have *nothing* to say.

Can you practice *that?* Can you *mourn* that, in all good faith?

No Other Heaven

Startled by the hectic shuffle of wings,
As if someone

Were pulling several knotted ropes
Over my roof,

I sit up in bed to listen, the night backing off,
As the blushed moon

Fades deeper, and is by now
Somewhere else,

Flashing in the almond leaves,
Ten thousand miles

From this one *sound* in the sea's light.

Later, in the afterthought
Of long rains, dark pools in the thin

Edges of dusk,
I'll remember, as I always do,

That one moment of separation,
(Something I should have done)

And the night,

                rushing in like a river.

But I don't want to think about
The irredeemable past.

Instead, consider the bright rose,

                        the choral odes,

In the *Paradiso*, cruising east —
With everyone else.

We're all heading straight into the tip of the orange sun,

Rounding the curvature of those dark brown hills,
On both sides, white fields,

Dry and waiting in the still-to-be light,
The cars behind me —

Linked to one another,

And to the right of the road —

A row of cypress, motionless, and to the left,
A weathered barn,

Sinking down into the earth's soil with every autumn.

The sun slants a little
Over the blue syllables of the sky.

How familiar it all is —

The words you chose to clothe your self in,
Those small props

That define your name when you first wake,

Are starting to wear
Like rain-beaten sign posts you pass each night,

Like a dream
Where nobody hears you.

Somehow,

This landscape with its trees open
Is an empty promise.

The birds, like tiny clusters of stars,
Have hurried away

To the one distance above me,
As though their secret were my own secret of sky,

And no other heaven.

Maybe Camus is right—that it takes ten years to have an idea of your own.

Maybe a lifetime.

A light rain blows in off the waves like a quiet verse.

How easily the heart hangs on.

If I close my eyes, a small wind will unlock me.

Thanksgiving

Dear Thomas,

Last night I followed the moon's path
above the cypress tree,
and up over the ridge of the sleeping girl's face
until it quietly vanished into the void.
I can't say if I heard the old tracks, the whistle and smoke
of *Eighteen eighty four*,
or was it the starlings, astonished
by their grief?
But it seems fair enough to substitute the moment for now.

I can't say how long the moon has traveled back and forth,
the same way, if it is worth
the trouble
like Sisyphus and his boulder. I can only tell you that by now
the eyes of so many birds are tired;
I would like to close my own,
and rest
the way the mallards rest on a cool pond.

November in the distance,
December with its axe, a blow to ice.
The clothes of so many bones,
gold teeth melted down,
stimulants for the heart, sedatives for the nerves,
and nothing less than the snow.

Wrong century. Wrong Deliverance. Wrong pocket of change.

Still, there is always the moon to consider,
shimmering a little in its watery flame, gathering the dark,

absorbing its grace, unencumbered,
climbing the sky in its black robe, slow
impartial pilgrim of the North.
I imagine the journey is more pleasant up there
than it is below;
more silent. Dear Thomas —

the work that awaits us is enormous.

The Drowning

Maybe it *is* all a matter of timing?

I had the dream again, *The Drowning*.
Only, I couldn't break through; the corridors were linked
to the moon's slow-churning water.

Not death, but transformation.

Thus tulips, wilted down from the hand of Jesus,
face buried in water, salt,

obedient servant,
the same archetypal sea, weeping,
the same lack of breath,

like a baptism I never asked for.

———

We believed you when you told us death would change us.
And that maybe the body of chaos rules the soul,
temporarily, from the slick cars that play havoc at earshot,
past the bare constitution of pines,

greenless, and seemingly hungry for a little rain.
But there was always the hope of reconciliation.
There were always the poets,

engaged with their hands,
flashing like flames through the stained-glass windows,
a muffled ache,

swallowed with a glass of wine.

———

One night, you stayed by the window
and watched the stars tick by in their invisible tracks,
like Bach's partita,
                    repeating the sound of Threes
as though that meant something.
And it did, to Pythagoras,
who learned the secret of harmonizing every atom in the body.
Just imagine the cells arranging themselves,
                              like the fine network
of a leaf,
the perfect key of silence.
And then I thought about that Buddhist priest
who could chant three separate chords,
                              simultaneously,
eyes closed, petals, folded.

                    ⸺

Days, years...
I wasn't looking for anything special
the time we drove all night to Key Largo,
not quite out of High School,
                    fishing gear tossed in the trunk,
Margo in the front seat,
                    rolling a number,
selecting the tapes, first Van Morrison, then The Dead,
and I remember the way the sea slept on both sides of the road,
the waves, flat and voluminous,
the moon,
          spread out like dazzling mica,

how was it possible to hate?
smoking another panama red beneath a palm tree.

I knew my politics back then,
from one shore to another, taking it slowly,

like a line in a verse that catches you off guard,
and then fails you.

So maybe it *is* just a matter of timing,
lost somewhere between the past and the future,
like a scarf tied to a branch,
                              a spin-off of verbs,

or a dream
in which you find yourself drowning.

Driving into Town with Franz Joseph Haydn

December sun in the cypress,
$\qquad$ climbing the hill of mist,

Haydn's concerto in the background,
illuminating the streets,
$\qquad$ the placid cars, the ordinary world

where the sun-tipped pines hold their attention.

And I imagined how inexorably bright he must have felt
when the strings sing above the average house,
like snow in the upper regions of the sky,

how he was able to reach that line of departure,
the *contrapunto, the finite,*
contrasting the parallel theme of the Absolute,
while I've been driving around the circumference of town,
lost for thirty odd years,
$\qquad$ in search of that *fixed point,*

the *Invisible Music.*

Back here, the neighborhood sky grows dark,
and the traffic builds with the hour,
as though we were all held up
in the preliminary flaw with time,

the cheap signs, the detour,
$\qquad$ the wrong turn at the wrong light,

crossing the tracks without looking,
avoiding each other as much as possible, or worse,

ourselves, on the verge of truth.

In the meantime, Haydn plays on,

so sure of his direction,
restoring the soul's health with dignity and grace.

Vincent Van Gogh's Mulberry Tree

And when the moon rose...
it lured me back to the branches, high air, thin as a girl's voice,
dark in the strangeness of December.
                                    The moon, like a secret,
monochromatic, changing grass into stone,
stones into light.
Day by day, we learn its secret, slowly. The taste of wine on a cold night.
The blackberries in autumn,
                            one at a time in clusters,
and the plum leaves drifting asleep in their purple shades.
Fog fills the valley with its spidery prayers,
                                    casting a spell on the heron,

hungry for the clouds to pass over.

Who can remember these things? You won't remember these things...
But I *insist*! Stroke by stroke, I *insist*!

What I wanted was a simple thing: the cicadas churning in the grass
are somehow more true than human desire.
The quiet crossing from water into night.
The damp violets, little purpling notes beneath the sunflowers.
The unexpected clouds, almost happy.

Thick blues, dazzling greens, left out all night on a hillside.

How odd you should forget these small attempts?
To degrade me for a handful of waste —
                                    the *shame* of it!

Metamorphosis

after Paula Modersohn-Becker

Fog light dripping in the eucalyptus leaves near morning.
You imagine the day as a small boat beached somewhere in the cold.
It takes a little more time to open your hands, to feel the light against
    the window,
More time. And then you see yourself as a young girl on a hill.
The trees are warm and immense, the sun is white in the edges
Of graceful shadows,
        and you are standing there with the sun
Defining your hair, and eventually, your thoughts.

For now, there are no particular transformations.
There is the spear-shaped leaf with its bark stripped down the branches.
The pale color of green gives way to black.
How many days will it take for the clouds to fade at the center?
Only desire repeats itself like the initial sound of rain,
The *tap-tap, tap-tap*, on the glass pane,
And the road, empty at the moment, of travelers, curving past the barn
And the blond wind blown back in a field.

When the doves settled in the light made of stone and wheat,
Lacking tenacity, you were ready to yield to a similar mood.
Not quite lonely, not ambitious for common habits or consolations,
Not fearful of the sorrows that pass like sleep,
Like a peasant woman who gathers hay in the first light
To feed the animals, who burns a fire, chops wood,
And says little, you were ready to tie the scarf around your hair,

And smell the coming of a harsh winter...
You would not wake up for a long time, *dove-dreaming*,
Poking a stick into flames.

Old Peasant, 1903

after Paula Modersohn-Becker

They are the silent occupants of a barely penetrable world.

Sometimes they sit with their eyes closed in the aura of birch,
Or else the geese will feed quietly behind them.
There are times when they resemble the disciplined posture of priests
In the wrong clothes,
But I paint them holding the stem of a poppy,
A red poppy—like the tiny glow
Of the soul, *barely penetrable.*
I am drawn to their sadness which binds them
To these fields, the purple summers.
What do they know that we don't know?
What feeling fails us?

You worked all the days of your life,
Breaking the soil like crusts of bread, tasting the seeds
That raised you.
You turned it up and packed it down like your fathers
Before you. What patience is this
That I am slowly learning?
Night after night, your mothers stared from the cottage windows,
The same endurance. Snow,
Spring and autumn—the season of ritual and prayer—
This crumbling soil through your lined hands,
This *daily* pilgrimage

I keep seeking in my own face,
Though I am learning slowly that feeling is everything,
Feeling is the main thing,

And *here* near the poverty of sky, dark wheat,
I am alone
For the first time,
As though I were truly able to feel my way back—

To the impenetrable.

Wood-Carved Horse in Autumn

Was it autumn when the Trojans lost their lives to the Greeks?
When they wheeled the beautiful wood-carved horse,
Twice as tall as the Trojan's fort,
Into the welcoming homes,
The opened gates, as a gift that would end the war?
Ah, such a miserable deception.

Even as a child,
It was the first story that impressed me.
They slaughtered old Grandfather Priam
And left him for the dogs,
Like pigmeat.
They raped the girls, enslaved their wives,
But when they dragged the little boy into the gold-dust air
For the final execution, a sound rose
With such pain, anguish, that no one could move,
Every bird, man, child, held still,
As the sound rose and circled the wind, a long
Way up, higher and over the blood-
Stained tides where it turned into a circling hawk
Above the hollow fortress.

This much I remember as a child.
And my mother who warned,
Suffering opens the eyes to truth...

But as I was saying,
Autumn is a season for reflection,
A road, winding down the coast,
Orchards, and many acres of wheat.

Inland, the cornfields stretch for hundreds of miles,
And I dreamed of green throughout the night.
Maybe it was the beginning of day, the afternoon?
Either way, I was lonely.

The hills curved like a slow bend, like the naked shoulders,
The golden summer of a girl asleep.
How I would like to walk that road between the hills
And the confusion of autumn.

I can't help thinking
What if the beautiful wood-carved horse
Had been a gift
Instead of that miserable deception?

The Empty Window

A tea kettle whistles on somebody's stove.
Now it's stopped. Now there is only the solitary
jingle of silverware. Leaves,
burning out.

Little by little, the mallards return to the lake.
The Grandfather clock strikes six,
as if the table, last night's empty glass of childhood
stories, were an illusion of peace.

This is how it is —
since our faith in words has vanished.

Of course, there was the night
when the stars were like tiny bells,
and the tambourine boats clanged in the wind
with their handful of nets

and for a moment, I believed
in the music of the night, that we were not alone,
staring at one another —
through the kitchen window across the yard.

So the old man prepares himself for another November.
The days are too brief for words. I see
his cigarette burn down like the last glow of coal in the dark,
like blue smoke.

The Last Village

I was late for the funeral. The slow
cars drove by, one at a time, through the rain and puddles.
It was not my own,
                     but someone I didn't know at all.

A complete stranger.

The young woman, in an elegant sweater,
                              hugging a loaf of bread,

follows the last car
up the single knotted road of a ruined village,
past the grove of cypress,
                    and down the hill on the other side of the isle,

like Athena, contemplating our loss.

———

A stone temple rises in the half-abandoned skies.
The Lighthouse
              flashes its years across the night.

But no Sirens of warning.
                     Perhaps a table in an empty house,

three carnations in bottled water.
An elder closes his eyes.
Rain fills a tin can,
              a brass cymbal,

and the basket of apples on the front step.
                              The newspaper remains folded

on the straw chair, rain-drenched.

What ever made us think we are here for the taking?

A man laughs out loud,
                              pours his friend another glass of wine —

it's just that simple.

Another Chance

6 AM at the edge of the long pier.
No one in sight for miles.
The sun floats up on the waves like a huge pink sail,
as if to say,
        "I'll give you another chance

to start over."

The light picks up the cigarette butts, the smell of rotting shrimp,
fish tails, scales, flakes glittering off the boards,
in the basin of rust and blood.
                  The same cheap hotel

stares at the changing clouds,
and all the voices are clambering out of bed,
newspapers smacking the doors, fathers —
ignoring their wives,
            children avoiding their parents.

(Romantic notion
buried on the lips of Keats,
           Rome — in somebody else's poem.)

The desire to say something pure,
unlike the gull's raspy screech, is a growing problem,

no matter how many windows you open,
the motherless children stand below, mute, and always
a little hungry.
        So you fold back the windy paper where you found it.

The front page of suicides and plagues
indelibly sketched on the waves of every century,
and later, justified, in the history books:
reductio ad absurdum.

The fishermen sleepily approach the dock,
low chatter, smokes, wool caps,

                         salty faces and hands,

coffee mugs, rods, tackle boxes,
buckets of small fish,
as if to say,

               "I'll give you another chance"

in the angled light, just breaking,

                      a few feet out...

Why Eros Will Not Return

In the pre-dawn hour,
before the willows have slipped through the light of wind,
before the mud-colored finches flit back and forth,
picking the dirt with their tiny hammers,
                                        before I can begin to consider

anything in this half sleep,
I put the water on for coffee,
wait in the kitchen,
                    try a few words,

in the attempt to chase the fear of emptiness,
temporarily, from the house,
when suddenly I see that the lamp above the table
has attracted a small, red-colored finch to the window,
its sharp nails scratch at the sill,
                            the threshold of glass

that keeps light and bird apart —
the way Psyche must have felt
when Eros would not return, night after night
in the coldness.

And maybe I'll accept the interpretation for the moment,
that you can love someone far more intensely
in the imagination
                    than in the dullness of habit,

that familiarity is the lowest form of knowledge,
spoiling the natural beauty of things.

And perhaps this is why Eros will not speak or come too close;
that is the condition.

But when Psyche disobeys and lifts the candle,
Eros flees, returns home,
                    leaving her like an orphan,

the longing for reconciliation,
as though she were seeing the grass without the green,
the sea without the moon,
                    the lake,

drained and emptied of darkness.

So maybe it's lovelier to always pursue than to possess.
Not that you have ever thought about me in this way,
and I have not been given the fate
                    to lift that candle:

Here is the unsayable landscape within us,

the leaves, the light,
                    the lake,

filled with the moon's desire.

Coup de Grâce

The *Nos* and *Absolutely Nots* are of no importance.
After all, the flower girl is practicing patience with her pink,
yellow roses, and red carnations,
like a parrot's wing,
     at the corner of 9th and L.

You wonder what the lilacs think
everytime the cars whirl by in a rush?
Well then, since I am man out of step with his world,
I'll buy as many as I can,
     and don't forget the orchids!

those lavender petals remind me of last night's sea
at the old harbor
with its boats anchored down like words on a page.
The tourists left for the day,
     and there was only the cook

outside the door of the café,
wiping his hands,
    and smoking a cigarette.

A moment comes when you stop asking for explanations,
when everything is as it *is*.
    The night winds down its silence

to a solitary sandpiper's cry —
so familiar and strange,
    (perhaps you haven't noticed?)

Tomorrow, the traffic will pass the flower girl again,
the buses and cars,
businessmen and workers, as if preparing themselves
for the grand illusion,

   the *coup de grâce*,

(attention diverted somewhere else),
like a train racing through the dark.

There are those to whom place is unimportant,
But this place, where sea and fresh water meet,
Is important —

THEODORE ROETHKE, "THE ROSE"

A Chorus of Rains

What gifts there are are all here,
in this world.

I.

The Buddha,
having realized all efforts are useless,
sat under a cloudy tree
and quietly lifted his eyes.
Dark settled down into his bones,
and the whole sky revealed itself
in the form of emptiness.

When the first clouds
take shape before the earth
turns within the sun,
and the stones, smooth as rain,
harsh, as an indictment,
become a winter road, *terra incognita*,
left under the moon, left to the crackle
of a thousand leaves, forgotten thistles
and a wind that freezes fire—

remember every god you've ever worshipped.

———

I remember once,
from the mountain of Salt Springs,
the pines, silent as a rose,
no one around, alone,

the sea in my arms —
one luminous pine, singled out,
as though the sun —
caught it — in a moment's flare,
but I swear to you —
the tree was, itself, its *own* light.

Who is left to gaze into the strange mantra of clouds?
       Who can say its name?

    2.

Some of us wake up to an empty house,
only to hear the same thin sound —
trapped in a sunless oak
and weathered
as our dreams
wheeling through the day and from the day
       to night,
while on a cliff-side, the moon, poised like a swan,
and the soul sings quietly to herself,
sad as a windless willow,
the soul sings quietly in the dark.

    3.

Autumn,
and I'd forget the battered silence,
the empty gestures, the dead tree in the *café*,
I'd forget the false order of possessions and the faces
       that belong to them,
the certainty of edicts and paradigms,
the investment of a life-long ritual.
I would leave my car to the street's racket,
and remember
something like — the damp smoke of an open fire,
burning in the autumn sea-swell,
alone, and not alone,

and the pines swaying from the dark hush
    of the earth.
I would remember
to sit silently
until the whole sky reveals itself
in the form of emptiness—
I would sing as quietly as a lark
at the low bend of *shivering bunchgrass,*
    and seed cones—
that impassable road you wrote about . . .

emptiness everywhere like a live thing.

Take Five

I'd like to be able to see our house —
the way I remember…
I'd like to open the door to my seven-year-old room,
northern sun unyielding through the window,

snow in the backyard.
I'd like to see my mother, making coffee in the kitchen,
my piano with its dreams attached to the cold.

I'd like to sit down
and practice that one difficult passage
because I know, as I knew then,

that I could seal it —

if my father hadn't gone away,
if we had stayed long enough into the future.

I think it's true to say that poets are frustrated musicians.

My mother played the sax in an all girl jazz band
and she was good enough to score the solos.
I remember how we'd sit by the fire,
flipping records, Stan Kenton,

Count Basie, *Take Five*…

"We were told not to play those pieces," she said,
"The manager asked us to keep it to dance,
But we'd always managed to slip one in just for ourselves.
He was right, they were made for the ears,
and not the dance-floor."

I don't know why that little conversation stays with me
like a squall of light welling up through the trees.
I think it's the image of dissolution—
how we lose the music for the cheap tune, the hubbub

across the dance-floor.

Los Osos Valley Road

There's a road that always catches my eye
when the light narrows off a slow pasture of cypress

and up to the barn
of stored wheat, oats for the cows and two horses.

The cars drive past and I drive past,
                                      too blind to formulate the answers,

to give back the wind its heart.

Still, something never fails to call me back

to its Rilkean winds,
                    its *hours before the rain,*

eroding the fence,
a shovel, rake, a silver pail, left out for the cat's milk
                                      and the one sad thread of light,

gliding across the wood pile.

You walk out with these aging trees and into the dazzling sun

as if the lies you spent your time rewarding

were the crimes of a petty thief,
                          ridiculous as a fool's trumpet.

It makes you ashamed, sometimes, to stand in the naked windfall.

Like these small bells, the sky's crows,

                    pedaling across the fields.

By evening,
the moon will appear in full dress,

               that slender stem of a rose,

that poor ballerina,
sulking in front of the window from her lover's note.

All I ever wished for is on this road: A tree, leaning in the winter rain.

Sycamore Bay

What is easy is difficult. It is so easy and difficult.
Like a game of tag where the only "home" is a tree on
the far side of the ocean.

FRANZ KAFKA

You are not quite there, yet.
But the wind has lowered its circles of gold
on a choppy ocean,
which would seem like a clue, or an angel's bracelet
burning just there — in the visible.

Someone down the shore kicks up the sand,
which blows every which way,
then stands fixed in a faraway space.

It's often difficult to take more than a few steps
into the bright memory of confusion,
to wait for the leaves to strike a balance —
so many miles before you.
It's easy to dream of the dream inside the dream
where something must give,
like an algebraic error where x is missing a y
to complete the equation,
and fall back again to the same brackets,
the blank parentheses,
begging the question from the void.

None of this is so easy, anymore. Even the clues,
when the clouds rush over the waves,
appear doubtful.

All the same,
I think I can see myself, somewhere out there over the waves,
or something like a shadow of myself,
beneath the half-darkness,
not desiring the metaphor for a change,
or the abstraction,
but simply the earth—in its turbulent beauty,
as though I were caught, *there*, in the grip of crosswinds,
there—on a small inlet that comes into focus
whenever the sun is slowly carried along on its skiff of tides,
as though it were always so easy to remember
things as they are—

like a tree on the far side of the shore.

Sleep

I think I remember it now...

The sun held still for a brief slow moment, and finally
you left down the cypress path.

The pregnant pause, the unspeakable summer.
                                        And then the leaves turned and turned,

snatched in the wind's torch.

Later that day, a mourning dove cooed from the wood pile. Sad bird.
I hear how you won your name.
                                        I hear the *hush*, the leaves, waving *so long*.

Soon the rains will appear in their grey and somber monk-hood. And
        the swallows,

they, too, will forget.

How I would love to undress this mask, the one

beneath desire, the one the Buddhists call, *Before your birth*.

When you were a child—the common declaration failed. *Ash to ash*, and then
        the snow

fell lightly from the trees like little Ps and Qs.
                                        Comforting, *no?*

Sleep on, then. Sleep on.

Logos

Someone is playing a concerto for guitar in the neighbor's garden.
If our world seems less coherent
than Vivaldi's,
like pieces of paper, shreds of light, suspended,
where the mind pulls upward,
we cannot blame it on perspective through the vacant dark.

Events still have their causes.

Like the figures who stand in a framework of white,
who appear helpless,
elsewhere,

almost abstract,
not in space, but in the full elaboration of meaning.
That's how the Greeks spoke, in any case,
for nearly a thousand years.

By the help of some god

they'd be caught saying.

And yet the daffodils
pursue some sort of diplomatic course
when they focus on the sun,
the blue regalia of the sun sifting down from *that* world

to the *other*.

If you listen long enough,
you can still hear it gradually fall
between the leaves
where the mind grows light with distraction.

Re-constructing Beauty

Beauty is the elusive moment of understanding.
DELLAS HENKE

Pink moon floating in the primitive dawn
where small waves crush the clattering shells back
and forth in the sand, deconstructing,
indifferent
to the elusive moment
that flares quietly twice when the sun strikes the leaves,
falling.

There is no objective truth —

only the dream re-appearing,
heaped, over there, in a tangle of weeds,
dry now in a mist of gnats from yesterday's sun,
deconstructing, so they say.

When snow petals fell in a different country,
Beauty waited from a brief distance
to seize the heart—
the C flat that Mozart touched,
reluctantly, on his piano,
from which an entire symphonic grace,
emerged in the rapture of one
intricate note,
on a bad night when the rain pronounced itself against the windows, sadly.

Perhaps most things *are* improbable:
The way we're drawn to a particular shape, the principle of form,
the eyes which focus on this pine to the next,

in the steadiness of light,
the way the blue-tipped jay *lends* itself to what skeptics call
begging the question,

what Keats called *Truth*.

Waters of the Sun

Each morning,
the sun washes over the same shore
in the ruins of small winds
up the banyan grove,
and leans there for a while,
bleaching the leaves Byzantine gold.
A bird lazily drifts across the sky—
and never returns.
Near the edge of the black-stoned graveyard,
waves weave the blue waters
of the night
into a veil of stars above the pastures.
All day,
I have been waiting for the moon,
the dolorous boat
where an egret is so still,
not even the horse's sweeping tail
can stir his poise
against the backdrop of these cliffs.
I want to walk out—
but fear the only path homeward.
The rain keeps soaking down the earth.
When did I start counting
the small dark stones along the waters
of the sun—
as though this were my last hope?

Magenta in Fall

After the trees surrendered to the sanctity of winter,

a renaissance of leaves bristled in the mist.

After the trees reconciled themselves to the night,

I shut the door—walked out,

                    as far as I remember,

unwilling to return to the small,

trivial habits that consume our daily lives…

———

And then again, what shame should be executed

by those in authority?

              The moon can be gracious if you let it—

the way the sea pulls the shore all night long.

Thus Odysseus could not bear to hear the sirens sing,

the darkness spreading sorrowfully,

                  centuries ago. The stars,

tacked to the night and somehow convincing

that the universe has opened a calm space for the bargain

we've made at birth.

                          Absolute mercy, a question in free-fall,

as we beg at the altar — that implacable faith,

rising and falling with the tides.

———

Because the wind, dazzling courage, would not relinquish…

because the moment she sliced the bread,

                                  and held the light, briefly,

on the outskirts of 1940,

                         the streets, stubbed out like ashes —

because the silence was everywhere,

                               rushing over the creeksides,

impatient, restless as vicious dogs —

                         because she could not possibly

imagine the flowers, drifting like tiny chimes,

apricot in May, magenta in Fall…

The Wager

For weeks now,
I've watched the field turn slowly
under the sea-tide,
absorbed in light, and the strange transition
of autumn.

The moon, for the time being,
is a heavenly priest—
one who is *in* the world, but not *of* it.
I would like to sit with him
in the cool horizon
and believe nothing else.

Back here, however, the soul keeps touching
the hands of the body,
the rectangular shapes of doors,
the corners of the window, the window, itself,
until it gains
some small recollection,
just a few yards out, where the poppies
flare their apricot skirts
under the bright weight of the sun.

The herons steadily pass without a single wing-beat.
The wind lowers its anchor of mist
along the rim of evening,
and the thin black trees keep a disciplined watch.

At Big Sur

Before dawn —
The moon gradually climbs the old constellations,
Making its pilgrimage above the waves.

Sharp cries of the crow mushroom up from the oaks
Where the blue-scented winds swell down into the canyon creeks,
Waking the eyes of the owls from the cabin window.

Sea-shuddering otters flash and float like slick rocks,
Burning in the nickels of haze and light,
The sea's persistence of erosion,
Blasting the coves, the winter shores.

And now the hawk,
Shifting and turning effortlessly above the cypress.
Sun, like a huge wild poppy —
Lost in a field of clouds.

Being

Does the road wind uphill all the way?
Right to the very end.
EMILY BRONTË

By winter, the deer vanished quietly with the grass,

like Rothko's *White and Greens in Blue* –

bare, empty, and somehow, vaguely familiar

with its sad pines following each other up the hill,

like a funeral, disappearing.

———

Parmenides argued that nothing exists except *Being*,

that the leaves, spoiled and wasted, in the wet flames,

are unreal, as unreal as desire, sensing the loss

of your own brief flight,

        as you get into your car, and drive on

with anxious predictability.

———

There is loss. And then there is *loss*.

There is the sweet scent of fresh bread baking on the *rue du Cherche-Midi*, Paris.

And you, waking to the rush,

and that the flute you hear from an open window

is constant and longing for nothing so absent as this wind,

invisible music.

———

Being and the many words that follow.

The vowels and sultry paragraphs,

forming its story of a meaningless world —

as habitual as any good Sunday:

the cars, the buses, the same drunk, begging,

everyone begging to sustain their weight

in the traffic and noise.

———

A man sits down in the company of his friends. Someone begins to talk,

mechanically. He glances over to the light,

(the laughter entering the room is not his imagination).

Something is beginning to slip from his hands,

the way the leaves slip from the elms.

———

Blackbirds churn the sky. No wind. Grey mist and a few drops of rain.

You pull off the road and stare gravely at the seagulls.

It reminds you of a scene in Italy during your travels in college,

as if you'd been asleep for twelve blank years.

You get into your car, and drive on

with unsettled predictability, a customary habit of the mind.

A heron sways above the willows.

Now it is beating its bright wings across the pastures.

This is how the soul distinguishes itself

from the endless hunger.

———

If only for a moment, *the scent of bread, the moon and the leaves...*

Simone Weil on Easter Morning

Easter rising.

Pools of fire in the wind-tipped pines where the owl still coos from the bay.

All the longing of pathos,
returning like a parable of grief.

Yesterday, the mustard flowers were just beginning to burn the hills
in thick Van Gogh-like strokes.
Orchestrated light, spilling over the rocks,
and the moon's rosette, still yielding.

The Gospels scattered to the winds.
Jesus, the Buddha, eyes closed, palms up, and the tree
that simultaneously bloomed
the day he awakened.

It is easy to understand this little death of the self,
how she had already left the boat, the daily news,
a bit of stale bread, untouched for days,
a candle, glued to the window —

how she turned to the tiny stars from inside that room
and quietly stepped into the night,
the way a girl slips from a dress,

the way the soul heals herself slowly.

Long Day's Journey

Listening to the wind last night in the twisted cedar,
the moon raking its leaves across a field,
owl, baffled by the cicada's chant,
        I could scarcely make out

the foghorn, flashing its mute notes across the waves.

And it reminded me of that sad woman's addiction,
a long day's journey into the night,
        the gull's hunger, its diligent

strife, untying the knot at the void's end,
the way the cars sleep on through the bright rain
in the middle of winter,
      luck's refrain,

blasting the metaphorical shore,
its irresistible waves,
      down and under, *down and under,*

like Dante's ghosts.

———

And isn't that what she wanted —
to forgive the pines,
     tipped in the wind's magenta?

Isn't that why she despised that lousy house
with its moan of decorum,
      its shelves of dust and pale doors?

Like the slow notes of the cello, the bitter rush,

late at the day's end.

October

is the month of lit fields and apricot-colored pumpkins,
the color of last night's moon, full
as a field of poppies,
>   swaying their jazz to the flashing stars—

a night when you'd rather surrender yourself
to the unexpected—
>   than fool the trumpet of judgment

with slick lies and ridiculous jokes.

(It reminds you of that Italian evening
when leaves bristled the shadowed streets,
when the rain gave in to *pentimento*,
which eventually ruined *Madonna and Child*
on the café's street.)

October is the month of deep blues and sweet pines,
whirling in a dervish dance.

The month Augustine fell to his knees,
>   and begged God to remember—

when birds follow the patience of leaves,
and roses fold like dark sonatas.
>   October—

when everything slowly falls to its knees,

quietly, and with exaggeration.

Morning Prayer

In the half light of the moon,

darkness sliding away from the hills,

I opened the door to the pastures.

The old mare stood beneath the cypress,

patiently waiting for her oats.

Everything covered with ice, the trees, the chairs,

the leaves, asleep, still drunk

from last night's frost. And again—

the red plume of the cardinal amid the erosion:

the shed and dilapidated fence,

the wheelbarrow, rusting in the sunlight.

I want to wake you from your morning dreams

before it all disappears into the mindless traffic.

To be in this moment is not in vain.

Let the world pass me by with its foolish ambitions.

I'm here, feeding the mare her oats—

as if nothing else mattered.

Futile Attempt

Everything is for you: my daily prayer
And the thrilling fever of the insomniac,
And the blue fire of my eyes,
And my poems, that white flock.

ANNA AKHMATOVA

And since the moon is drunk tonight,
and walking around in the fog like somebody's lost beloved
with her arms, bristling with silver,
and a white shawl thrown back,

I'll go down to the dining room table,
and join her for a glass of wine.

And maybe, if the night permits,
I'll listen to the sea's balalaika, a slow Russian folk song,
sad as a peasant's heart,
lapping the hem of the shore.

A lament, *salute!*
to the one who walks straight through me,
shadows of hands in the dark.

And because I find it hard to sleep in the cold,
I'll sit by the dining room table, light the candle in the Spanish lamp,
and write something out of this darkness,

futile attempt.

Hanalei Bay

I could have easily stayed all summer,
lulled by the waters,
                taking the long way out to sea

when the tides rush slowly in,
tipping the waves magenta, upshore
from the trees.
            I could wait for the rain

to diminish this spot like a last chord,
easily, and without regret,
                but something out there in the shifting light

breaks you,
and so you row a little closer to the shore.

A small breeze unbraids the bamboo, exaggerating its brilliance.

Let it fall with the waves in a downpour,
effacing the thread of rocks,
                and the sun's loose claim to grief,

where fishermen walk the reefs, outside of time.

Birds turn *again* and *again* like hand-written notes,
scattered against a green sky.

Maybe we're here, just once, to remember these dazzling pines,
and the hush of waters,
            and the low blue clouds

just barely touching the sea?

Maybe there is no final enlightenment,
                                        no promise of heaven —

only the moon,
a sailboat skirting the harbor, the flurry of birds

in the sure ease of the heart.

Korinthiakòs Kòlpos

Days of luminosity. Faithless sea of milky blues and white roofs.
Time to push back the shutters, burn the candles, open the bottle of wine.

What do I love about this island? The music of erosion, old ritual
of a fisherman's boat, nets knotted by hand.

What do I love about these tattered houses that step out from the
      19th century—
that peer at us like strange invaders,

as if we were wrong to improve upon their ways?

I want to row in to your quiet whitewash, your black & white shuffle
of outdoor cinemas and cards slapped down with a laugh.

I want to row out a little farther from the pier—just there—
where imperfections, flaws and filth,

become a flame of something timeless, the way an old woman
crosses herself, tossing a handful of salt

for the Lady of Sorrow.

Perhaps it's only that bare tree that makes me dream of such music?

Grapes, cicadas, sea, wine...
The moon makes a bold appearance—

as if there were nothing to hide.

Three

We suffocate among people who think they are
absolutely right, whether in their machines or in
their ideas...

ALBERT CAMUS,
Neither Victims Nor Executioners

Those who left were like family. We missed them.
The ones who came back were complete strangers.

YANNIS RITSOS, "CHANGES"

Whoever is uprooted himself uproots others.
Whoever is rooted himself doesn't uproot others.

SIMONE WEIL

They are writing down their life
on a century fallen to ruin.

ANNE SEXTON

September

and all of its singular regrets
                    half-opened.

September
and the trees lean into a poor rain.

September
and I'm beginning to feel the pull of bones,
                                   my own perpetual darkness,

an intimation from the leaves —

Nothing has really changed from the last parting.

The elm continues to shuffle back and forth.

Outside,
the crows line up and acknowledge their thin shadows,
                                        at ease with the dark.

Everything in a temporary stand-still,
everything lighter,

as if the soul could weather the endless rain.

Los Desaparecidos

A wild sun floats over the sea of Isla Negra.
The waves return again and again to the hollow caverns.
You used to see it all from this window.
Here are your shells, your colored bottles,
a few lines written in haste.

They say the shot that killed your friend, Allende,
did not stop short of Salvador's heart,
but entered your own,
silently.

The birds slowly rose against the autumn sky
where the bells could not be heard.

Today, two ugly, high rise apartments face your cottage,
defying a butterfly's wings,
the fishermen, making the sign of the cross,
a beautiful girl, lifting a basket of fruit to her hip.

There was a time when the children laughed down this road
on horseback. Their fathers,
simple peasants who worked the land,
were labeled "Leftists,"

"Communists," and then they disappeared, all at once.
Fathers, sons, the holy ghost...

And again, the birds rose by the thousands.
Unseen, untold—and without end.

Dead leaves are falling through the winter air.
There must have been a moment of hope,

before *los fusilamientos* raised their rifles and pinched out
the sea's light—

Such a long way from your home, Pablo Neruda.

You cup the shell to your ear, *close your eyes.*
How softly the bell tolls...

Lost Child in the Painting

Winter approaches with its sad eyes,
                    its windows of faceless children

and wounded pines, where a solitary rake, and a turned-up pail

weep in the falling snow.

Church bells slip through the barbed-wire fence,
                    through a dog's jaw like frostbite.

Everyone's gone, nothing's left but a boy's boot, its tongue torn out in
      the snow.

How is it possible to cure their hate, our pain
at the hands of executioners?
                    A conspiracy of fear,

and the machinery of death.
A warehouse of slaughtered children. Such a small girl:

A trifling.

One child following the other...
                    "until the end justifies the means."

Consider this painting of the girl at the window,
posing in the summer light,
in a blue dress,
                    with small, white daisies in her hand.

It once belonged to a Jewish family—somewhere on the outskirts of Germany.

Now it's for sale, after forty-five years of confiscation.

Such a delicate face,
like the parents' child who was mutilated by the German soldiers.

A trifling.

Would you care to dine at the old café where they seized the infamous artist?

Shall we discuss this—*rationally?*
                              the way we murder, *rationally,*

with clean gloves and white masks?

Watching Gregory Peck in *To Kill A Mockingbird*

with the moon washing away the careless trees
from his front porch,
the leaves, stiff and raked aside,
in late summer;
how graceful Gregory Peck looks
when the unnoticeable wind catches his focus,
the way the moon sadly sinks
on its knees
in a quiet yard, and the neighbors have left you

the illusion of salvation.
This is the road that diverges to the poor
and impoverished, it tells you,
do not forget us
when the machine, the lynch mobs, burn their cross,
our worthless bodies. Do not forget
to explain the laws,
the semblance of justice, to a man who stares all night
into a prison wall, dead weight of his
arm, anchored
like a mental burden.

And only later, late in the evening,
as the darkness falls
like a slow ache you've grown accustomed to,
will you hear the mockingbird
sing on the higher branch of the trees,
outside your window,
repeating the heart's grief,

allowing the knot of execution
to hang above you,

like a cloud, white and still,
on a clear morning.

Gregory Peck, as Atticus Finch,
takes the road less traveled, across the tracks,
to the driven out, deprived,
the exhausted shelters,
to feel his way, slow and empty, in the skin
of another man's hopes,
to keep faith.

But this is a world that valued customs more than conscience

in a room full of contrast:
the fortunate,
fanning the heat away,
and the poor,
who are forced to bear witness
from the upper chambers
of the court.

(*So many days before us,*
sweet Jesus,
so many years to shake off)

And when the film is over,
I imagine Atticus,
timeless as the moon memorizing
his place
on his front porch, the drowsy breeze of jasmine,
crickets churning their rattles
in the nightgrass.

I keep him there —
(click) just so.

for Gregory Peck

At the End of the Day I Listen to Bach

Sunday again,

and as usual, the morning fog

unrolls its white sleeves,

the days sleep on like an old dog in the distance.

The same story—

the waiting.

From the bay, the last rows

of eucalyptus trees

stand out

like quiet disciples,

spinning their prayer-wheels into the cruel sun.

I imagine the house, empty.

Lights on.

Little pieces of wind

burning blank notes across my window,

knowing by now—

you are somewhere else,

the rain sinking in,

the moon—

tipping the leaves

in all the colors of magenta.

Rain, fog, the house filled up

with small deceptions.

The letters

in neat stacks. The parapet

and the trumpets.

The man gesturing

in the telephone booth.

The women in line, flipping the pages back…

Excess,

warned the Greeks—

is the black step of isolation,

the fallacy

inside the Fallacy, unwinding,

as though it all made perfect sense.

(And why did you struggle with those words?

Blake—

the only thing that mattered...)

How beautiful,

to possess meaning, looking up to the clouds,

inseparable,

some mysterious part of you,

outside it all,

like listening to Bach,

the insistence of Form,

each note, an integration,

each note, a prayer-wheel turning,

waiting.

Quiescent, dark.

From the Other Side of the Night

Maybe it's true that the nights are merely a temporary shift of color?

I can't say what was going through her mind,

my mother at the window,
                                    washing the same dish for 15 minutes,

mesmerized by the snow's hush in the red pines,

as if the body were left momentarily
                                    to its mechanical strings

and the soul rose out of its frame like a cool rain in the open light,

a flurry of geese tipped like a thousand candles—

until something snaps,

                        like a parachute, and all the squares of acreage

grow larger and out of focus,

the sad narration of forks, spoons and left-over words,

propped up and waiting on the table,

                                    like a Chekhov play.

—

Some of us simply tip our hats to the door,

like P.B. Shelley in his storm-lit boat, like Socrates,

raising his cup of hemlock,

much like that character in Bukowski's *Barfly*,

toasting cheerfully,
> *To all my frien-n-n-n-nds!*

with one last swig and then he buried the axe for good.

Did he actually believe he was going from here to the Intelligible?

And why did he hope to meet with Agamemnon?

Did the hemlock rush to his brain—
> or just to his heart?

In any event, he died, feeling a whole lot better without us,

leaving his body to the women to wash, and the sun,

crossing the Acropolis,

> Apollo, in a dome of trees.

———

Time forgives no one,
> not even Agamemnon's cruel thrust,

forcing himself into the frightened slave girl,

Achilles' loss.

———

In the distant field,

    a chorus of silence,

in the distant rock,

    a chorus of ruin,

in the distant trees,

    a chorus of slumber,

in the distant wind,

    a chorus sings of ghosts.

———

Some nights,

    when it's clear you've left forever,

when everything slows down long enough to feel its grief,

burning like the morning's river,

    I let the dark fall upon the sweet grass, inch by inch,

I let it fall and fall until the rain gives up,

until the night proves otherwise.

It's like a tide that takes you in,

                            always out and farther away

than the playful yelps of the seagulls.

Whatever you see is lost to a bit of sky, a field of ambiguity,

the window that faces north,

                            the *perhaps* of some distant moment…

cold as November's stars.

The Night Russia Vanished

after Anna Akhmatova

I remember the trees
and how the snow lit up the night from the train's passage.
I drank tea. I smoked.

The trees flashed, once, twice and then...*nothing.*
Or was it the muffled coughs
between the tracks?

The gentleman seated across from me —
lost everything: the poised stare, the paper, the gloves.
The living. The dead. The wasted talk.

There was Alexis' Brahms, filling the stifled air of the parlor —
his long slender hands desired more,
something *unattainable.*

I loved him for that — for forgetting.

He's fallen asleep again.
Better to sleep than to smoke and think.
How strange — still young, still slight

against the falling snow. As pale
and deep as the snow.
An empty glass, and suddenly your days

are as remote and opaque as the moon's emigration, the Balkans.

Terror always begins like a beautiful requiem:
the parades and cheers and little waving flags easily
seduce you.
And then it happens almost over night:

The loud abominable fists at your door. The arrests
for no reason. And our submissiveness,
those prison gates,

stark and helpless as our God.
That night, Mandelstam
was taken away into the night.

By spring, the bees plundered the buried sun.

I can't remember how many evenings we spent—
the lamp-light flowing down inside the café's smoke
where it was safe to read a few lines of verse.

I only remember the trees, now. Bare. Black. A blur
against the window's passage,
the private moments, disappearing—

Leningrad: city of exile. No past.

Privileged

Winter trees, brooding, self-absorbed.

    The slow bright spot lost in the yellow leaves,

and the birds that rush from the rooftops.

    I dreamed of the sea in early summer

before the tourists made their deadly rounds.

    The composition of the day, ruined.

Tables, chairs, newspapers folded neatly.

I envy their measured lives—

    the bicycle, propped against the trellised wall,

the café, and its happy jingle of silverware.

    I'm talking about the wine taken for granted

when bombs shatter your neighbor's house,

    and all you want is a glass, a candle—

anything that vaguely resembles

    the habits that keep you grounded

when there is nothing left for you to do

    except wait, and smoke,

crouched in the corner of the hallway,

    until the clarity of light lifts its ugly mask:

How noble art thou...

This morning,

    I woke up thinking of Chekhov,

pouring his afternoon tea,

    the cherry orchards,

shimmering in the wet sun.

    Perhaps it explains that dolorous note, right at the end,

that sad string, plucked,

    like so many leaves, falling,

and that even the first blow of the axe—

    cannot reach the wound

that heals us.

Kafka and Milena

A full moon glimmers on the water.

The air is dark and the branches are just a brushstroke.

When he finally arrived, tapping softly in the hallway,

he didn't know what to do—what to say.

Her shoulder was bare and beautiful in the moonlight.

He pressed his lips, *there* and *there*.

> *I can't, Milena. I can't…*

Later, after the Nazis confirmed his nightmares,

Milena continued to write,

a communist against the Germans.

Her father could not restrain her.

The child, the morphine, the disciplined heat…

That year, she was trucked to a concentration camp. She died

the way Kafka died, tormented. Anguished.

The moon is wide and its petals are falling

within the garden.

The dark wet scent of wheat

is a path of stars, a girl, surrounded with pleasure.

This time, he takes her as shyly as night—

without the warnings or premonitions.

                              Words blur, vanish.

One impossible choice—and suddenly—fate is determined.

Small Tree

after the photographer, Albert Renger-Patzsch

Perhaps it's the absence of color that draws him near to this tree.
It is small, thin, and like a stark crow —
it waits for no one.
There is a white field and a white sky
turns beneath the branches.

The first rains have not yet come. And yet
it is winter. There is no sound from the distant
shots, or the hospital filled
with the wounded...

Not a breath of wind, no birds or perpetual smoke
from the empty houses in the village.

Perhaps he imagines the sky as a frame of silence?
The tree, a sort of contrast, a line
drawn with chalk.
He has waited a long time to find this tree,
alone, in a somber moment.
Imagine the moon—as he adjusts the lens,
his subject focused into deeper light so that it's almost dark
a few yards back from the branches.

Is it not like a small boat,
drawing us close to the shore?

for Michael Kinsley

Remembering Giotto

After all, the night could only afford a little rain
through folds of light,
and who could argue with the sleep-walkers,
climbing back into their cars,
                              like clock-work?
Or Blake, for that matter,
who painted Newton under the ocean.

————

All morning I watched the long-billed Dowitcher
pull across the lake,
the flat surface, with its glass of dualism,
played the sun like music
                              from a different age.

It still captivates us —
Giotto's blue sky and leafless tree,
                              distinct from the burning-
away-angels.
Less clear than a memory, anyway, of failure
and sickness of heart.

The way lovers will imitate the lost summer
of darkness,
                  the slow rise out of the self,
unhealed —
for the time being,
                    (fog lamp in the pepper trees,
and all the corners of the fresco.)

But it's hard, sometimes, to settle for anything less.

It's hard to remember
     not to take it all for granted.

So I look, for the rest of the morning,
with my binoculars focused on the purple finch,
         the poppies on fire.

The gulls begin their ballet in grand strokes.

         Now all at once,
they have risen together, floating slowly upward,
closer than I imagined to Dante's angels,
        closer than I imagined

to light.